The Promise of a Grander Tomorrow

By: Benny R. Ferguson Jr.

The Promise of a Grander Tomorrow
By Benny Ferguson © 2014

ISBN:
978-1-7354117-1-2

Published by:
The Ferguson Company

Editor & cover design:
http://roxanec.wix.com/time-to-read.com

Introduction

It is said that you never truly get what you want in life. It is said that you must be realistic when it comes to your goals and dreams. Who exactly says such things? Do you hear individuals who have lived enormous lives saying this, or do people who have struggled with disappointment make such bold claims?

What if there was a way to guarantee your success? What if there was a way that was within your grasp, closer than you think, that solidified your place in the history of individuals who accomplished all that they desired? What if it cemented your name in the ancient scrolls of individuals who had magnificent relationships, fantastic health, overflowing finances, a never say die mentality, and a connection with your Source envied by the holiest of holy?

Well, you can. The answer sits behind the idea that you must know exactly what you want in life in order to ever dream about accomplishing it. What do you want, in its true essence and form? What do you want? Why do you want it? What does it look like, sound like, feel like, smell like, and taste like?

At the moment there are only a few who know what they truly want. The mind of the masses is filled with the reactionary state and focus of all the things that it does not want. It is at present being blown back and forth by the winds on the ocean of life experience without an anchor of any kind.

If you truly want to navigate your way through life, if you truly want to sail the seas, visiting beautiful locations, making connections and relationships that are all of your choosing, you must realize the power of an "Ideal."

I introduce you to what it means to have an inward approach to life and business. I introduce you to a power that has been yours all along. I introduce you to what it means to stake your claim in the experience of life and how it changes the game.

3

The Promise of a Grander Tomorrow

I hope you are ready!

Anything and everything you can envision in your mind can be achieved and manifested. As a matter of fact, the minute you begin to view it in the eye of your mind you begin to draw it to you. All of the necessary resources are at your disposal. Situations and circumstances align in your favor. Obstacles appear to be in front of you but they are really only trying to get out of your way.

The question is can you hold your focus long enough? Can you sharpen the vision clearly enough? Can you feel its energy strongly enough to force its manifestation?

This is the power of an Ideal. It begins as a simple thought. It grows into an idea. It proceeds into a multifaceted component with many moving parts. And finally it morphs into a grand organism, encompassing and connecting many other parts to life solidifying its purpose and reason for materialization. It is radiating energy and life, and your passion and love for it, your desire feeds it as it grows non-physically toward materialization.

You are the catalyst. You are the farmer of the healthy Ideal that looks to present itself as a part of your life experience.

Benny R. Ferguson Jr.

The Understanding

To come to grips with the absolute possibility and potential that you wield in your life, you must first understand that you are solely responsible for your life. There is no out, no escape from this truth. While the masses cast blame and responsibility outside themselves, onto other people, the economy, the color of their skin, and the most powerful, beings and entities in the unseen, you can make the decision right now to explore and experience the fact that you are responsible for your life. You are living your life from the inside out, and the minute you begin attempting to prove this to yourself, you run into the first line of defense to your taking full control, your habits.

We are not talking about habits as in the ones you can see. We are talking about habits you cannot see. We are talking about how you think and how you feel on a regular basis. These are what give insight into the beliefs that are guiding your life from a non-physical, unconscious position.

When you begin to look into what you say and how you say it. What you feel and why you feel that way, you begin to see that you do not even think about the majority of your behaviors. The majority of your behaviors are merely reactions, unconscious, instantaneous reactions, which you have programmed into your mind as the necessary response to these particular situations.

If someone cuts you off on the highway what is your typical response? If your children appear to be disrespectful, what is your typical response? If there is a mistake with your paycheck, what is your typical response? These responses occur as if on autopilot, as if there is no other choice. This simply is not true.

A good question to ask is, "Do the responses that I normally display when events in life happen to me take me closer or away from my goals or what I truly want out of life?" Things like greater relationship with your children, spouse or partner. Is the response going to end in a win-win situation or is someone going to get hurt?

5

These are things that we very rarely consider, but yet are firmly within our control if we understand that we are meant to be in control of our minds and all of its activities.

Totally Committed

To begin the process of changing your mind you must first be totally committed to the change. Many provide lip service but are not truly ready to commit. And when I say commit I do not mean to give up everything that you thought was important to you, or to let go of things that you love.

To be totally committed means to commit to the process of readjustment. This is an awesome process. A process that is full of joy, exponential growth, and self-revelation.

The process consists of:

1. Recognizing where you are now as a human being;
2. Crafting out an image of who and what you want to be;
3. And consciously, on purpose choosing to be that person as often as you can remember, simply adjusting when you recognize that you have strayed.

This is being totally committed. This is what begins to place you in the big leagues in the game of life. This is what sets you up for entry onto the playing field of the elite.

In The Mind First

Everything that is occurring or happening in your life you have seen in your mind first. To connect with the onslaught of life and its constant presentation of occurrences you will begin to remember your thoughts. You will remember that thought about an aunt or an uncle and they called a week later. You will remember that you said you wanted a certain pair of shoes and a month later you came across them in a store marked down 50%. You will remember that you thought about a particular type of food this morning and around lunch time a coworker gifted you that very thing out of the blue.

These types of events happen all the time and yet you do not realize it because you do not remember your thoughts. Since the beginning of time master teachers have told you to look inward for understanding and power. They have reminded you to gather your thoughts and place them on things of the most high. Doing this places you in alignment with the good of the world and takes you out of alignment with the not so good. Doing this places you in a higher energy state, a greater mental attitude conducive to the type of life that every human being truly desires.

Trade It All

What would you give to experience the life that you truly want? What would you trade?

To get that which you truly desire in life, there is a trade necessary. The trade consists of you knowing, focusing on, and speaking of only that which you want. This is the second challenge because you are taught to speak mainly in terms of what you do not want from those closest to us.

If you listen closely you will hear it all around you. You speak about what you do not want in relationships. You speak about the negative and disappointment in your finances. You speak about the issues and challenges with your health, and I understand that it all may be true, but you do not get out of a situation by focusing on it. You get out of a situation by focusing on what you want it to be like versus what it is. This is what forces doors to open and resources to reveal themselves, which allow you to walk out into new, more positive, better circumstances.

The Mistake of Asking

The mistake of asking is that you do not ask in the present tense. If you want something, it means that in the present you do not have it. If you are striving for something it means in the present you do not have it. If you would like something it means in the present you do not have it, and all of these leave you in a state of wanting because in your mind you are without that which you desire.

The proper code to unlock the doorway to that which you want is to see it in your mind's eye as if you already have it, experiencing it now.

These delicate, subtle changes in thinking are what make profound changes in experience.

You want to experience a beautiful relationship. You want to have a healthy body. You want to have a fulfilling, challenging, rewarding job or career. You want to experience wealth and abundance.

Now how do you feel? You feel like you are without all of these things. No doubt you have tried to reach them, accomplish them, but you were unsuccessful. You were left feeling helpless, out of control, lacking in resources, abilities and capabilities to reach your goal, and the truth is that when you started on your quest this is how you felt.

Repeat these statements out loud to yourself.

I only experience beautiful relationships. I have a healthy body. My job or career is fulfilling, rewarding, and challenging. I am wealth and abundance.

These statements carry a completely different feel. "I AM" statements begin the process of placing you in alignment with that which you want or desire. These statements may feel uncomfortable at first because you may not truly believe them, and I ask you, "How can you ever have or accomplish anything you do not believe you can have or are worthy of?" You cannot.

8

"I AM" statements force you to come to the point of belief. They simultaneously force you to view the image of what you want in the eye of your mind and for a brief period of time see it as if it is in the present, existing now.

Coming To Grips

Coming to grips with the facts of responsibility, coming to grips with the obvious nature and fact that you are creating your experience as the evidence begins to present itself to you, can be a challenge.

There are so many misconceptions. There are so many unknowns in this world and beyond until you begin to tune your mind and your attention to the obvious reality that exist inside of you.

Time can be a challenge but it is not without its strong points. If you knew all, your existence would not be necessary. The learning of potential strengths that you have realized within yourself to this point have all served to grow your inward personal power, if you are astute enough to learn the lessons from your pains, or at least ask and wait for them.

Coming to grips is necessary for the engagement of the true power of your being. You are a non physical being, and your power lies in your thinking and in your feeling. These two faculties form and change the unconscious beliefs that drive your life.

Coming to grips with the possibility, is to finally agree with yourself that your life is not what you set out for it to be. You have not reached the levels that continue to call you from the deep recesses of your being. You do not know how to move forward or what you are missing in your quest to find purpose and meaning. You are lost in a sea of happenings, situations and circumstances. Your feet, mind, and body are in a tumbling whirlwind, and you do not know how to put them down in balance to go your own way.

Coming to grips is to find the ground, finally. It is to assume the role of the coach of your life, calling the plays, shuffling and maneuvering players, hiring new players and letting some go, all in the name of approaching your personal desires, successes and achievements.

You are the only one endowed with the power to do this in your own life, and you must take up the reins to truly move your life forward.

Unmistakable

It is unmistakable and undeniable that thinking comes first. The unconscious mental pictures, images, conglomerates of ideas are what guide your life. You do not think anymore. You do not choose or decide anymore. You merely react and respond to life and its many projections into your life experience.

It is unmistakable that you have lost your ability to think in a world that is made up of thought images materialized physically.

It is unmistakable that you have lost your bearings as to where your control lies in this thing called life. Do you control events after they happen or can you manipulate what happens before it happens? These are deep questions whose answers can be found and realized individually and personally, and they must.

Do you set your day? Do you set what and how you want it to unfold? Do you set your relationships and all other human interactions? Do you set their feel and the outcome desired from them? Do you set the parameters for your safety and your health? Do you choose the outcomes, the levels of performance and production that you require of yourself on any and every given day? Do you choose the power of the relationship between your spouse or partner and your children? Do you continue to succumb to low, negative images of self-value and worth? Are you an active participant in your life or merely a victim?

If you can be honest you are at the door. You are at the door of new possibility. You are on the verge of realizing your limitless potential. There is a crest above the moon, the darkness of lack of control, pain, and frustration has ended because now the sun of change is beginning to rise and has the ability to chase all of the looming shadows away, but there is one more thing you must do. You must assume the role of captain. You must take the wheel of your life. You must begin calling the shots, plotting the course on the inside, in your mind, and declare it so without compromise.

Life poses no objection. It willingly and gladly conforms. However, the physical arena of time and space that you live in causes a lag of time before materialization. Also, as it is your thinking, the images that are the first cause of your experience, it is also your thinking, the images present in your mind that must be countered, improved, replaced on a continuous basis to permanently change your experience. Conscious choice in thinking must be made unconscious.

Let's explore.

Becoming

The Challenge of Your Past

The challenge of your past resides in the many events that define you. The hurts, the pains, the disasters, the successes, the triumphs, the overcomings, all the messages stated and implied that you believed and continue to believe unconsciously that you received as a child.

They have molded your life into its present state. In large part it is full of things you do not like, and this brings the necessary question of why and where did it come from; surely you didn't choose this path. Yes, you did! Unconsciously you are calling to life all of your experiences through the thought patterns, beliefs and emotions that are the normal activity inside of you.

What do you want to experience? Were the events in the past true for everyone in the world? Did those loved ones around you, whose beliefs you hold dear, live powerfully effective, resourceful, successful lives as a result of their beliefs about money, health, relationships, and spirituality, or did they experience pain and disappointment?

You can turn the table with a change in your inner mental processes, a change in the way you think feel and act. You can change everything with a consistent conscious effort to become that which you want to experience. Yes, become that which you want to experience. See it, feel it, smell it, taste it, hear it all in your inner experience as if it is happening right now. This is what you must do.

When you start believing in the person, the things, and the experiences that you want in your life, the old beliefs, thoughts, and emotions begin to fade because you no longer give them the energy of life they need to preserve and exist non-physically.

The challenge of your past reminds you of all your shortcomings and the shortcomings of others, and if you continue to believe in the failures of people, non-physically you align yourself with that segment and continue to meet them in your life.

Happening All Around You

The life that you are creating exists and is happening all around you. It is in the people that you meet. It is in the stones on the street. It is in whether you get stopped by all the stop lights or whether they are all green. It is in whether you come in contact with angry or pleasant experiences. It is in whether you are the recipient of random gifts and charity or misfortune.

All of this is your life, it is happening all around you, and a simple shift in thinking, in what you believe, begins to mold a completely different experience for you.

Do you wish to meet kind, caring people in your world? Intend to do that. Do you wish for behaviors conducive to health? Intend to do that. Do you wish for your relationships to be better in your intimate and working life? Intend for them to be so. Do you intend for your finances to grow and the comfort level in which you experience life to increase dramatically? Intend for it to be so.

With these intentions you begin to engage the only factor, the only person who is responsible, the only person that you can control, and that is you.

You set your sights on a particular goal and begin the necessary changes on the inside to match up with that goal, with that experience.

The Resistance

The resistance to all that you desire is the intent of the maker of illusions. The illusions are your past limitations appearing real in your present. Keep in mind that your limitations and beliefs and life, the world, and what is possible are not true for everyone. So are they true limitations or are they just constructs of your mind?

13

This simple consideration keeps you centered and questioning the ideas that are in your mind, which serve to stop you when you have an idea or want to attempt something new that takes you out of your present comfort zone. Comfort has never been the true nature of the human being. Although the masses try to hide it, mask it, or have simply been trained out of it, those who have broken free have scaled the highest peaks, they have run the fastest race, they have traveled to distant lands, and you must do the same on the inside to begin molding a new life and discover the possibility that has always been present around you.

Arrange a meeting of the minds closest to you. Take an inventory of the thought processes. How many are pushing their boundaries? How many are reaching for the next level in any area? How many are envisioning new landscapes on this planet called Earth, or are they satisfied and comfortable where they are, settled into their daily routine, destined to carry them to their graves?

It is difficult to break free from the accepted thought process around you until you choose to break free and begin to challenge that thought process.

All you know is what is in front of you. You disregard the fact that other human beings are experiencing life differently and that the only difference is in your mind and how you think and view the world.

This is where the resistance ends and where possibility begins.

The Choking Point

The choking point of all who endeavor to change their stars, their present lot in life, is their ability to focus and stay focused on a goal until the resources, and necessary combination of situations and circumstances appear in time and space for the manifestation of the goal.

You have the ability to focus on an idea to the exclusion of all other thoughts and concepts, but you must cultivate this skill. To this point, the mind wanders, it jumps, it leaps from thought to thought from area of life to area of life, it believes, it does not believe, it is tossed to and fro by the events that happen outside of the body.

To begin focusing on an idea you must begin to disregard and exclude the happenings outside of you. You must begin to train yourself to believe only that which you choose to believe and develop on the inside.

The outer world is predicated by the inner world, and to cultivate the ability to focus on an idea, a situation, or a desired circumstance, is the first skill of a master.

How bad do you want it? If you want it bad enough then make it the first thing, the only thing you think about.

We do it all the time by default, mostly in the direction of things we are nervous about, worried about and fearful of. Our thinking gets polarized by an idea as we do everything we can to try and avoid a particular situation or circumstance, and we do everything right. Except for the fact that we have channeled our focus and energy toward what we do not want versus what we do want. This is a mistaken use of your power.

Focus is the choking point, and we focus all of the time. Notice what you are focusing on at the moment in every area of your life. Are you focusing on what you want to happen or what you do not want to happen?

Common Sense

A common question to creation is, "How to tell if what we are doing is correct or yielding our dreams in the making?" The answer is,

The Promise of a Grander Tomorrow

"Creation is in the light that you see in the emotion you feel. Creation is in the thoughts you create in your mind." New thoughts around your goal will appear, thoughts you have never considered before. They will be thoughts of glory, thoughts of triumph. They will be thoughts of power, thoughts of accomplishment.

Tonight, in the deep recesses of your mind, take a moment to consider that which you have long desired. It could be a situation, a circumstance. It could be a particular thing like a car or a house. Consider it, walk through it, feel it, smell it, taste it, hear the sounds that it will produce in your physical reality. Make it as real as you possibly can. Experience it as if you have it now.

Do this a few times a day and you will notice that you begin to attract resources, ideas, circumstances in your life that are associated with or similar to that which you are envisioning in your mind.

This is your activity all through the day. It is almost never ceasing. You think about relationships in a certain way. You think about people in a certain way. You think of yourself and your health in a certain way. You think about your partner, your spouse and your marriage in a certain way. You think about your finances in a certain way. You feel as though you are a creator, supremely powerful in your life or you feel as though life has you hostage, a victim and that you have little or no control.

In each of these you see yourself experiencing life in a good or a bad way, a negative or a positive way. You feel the love and bliss of possibility or you feel the weight of necessity. You hear beautiful songs of joy and abundance or you hear the negative talk of pain and discomfort. You see your life before you in your mind, and it is here where the magic begins. It is here where the fusing of the particles of life begin to come together to culminate into a physical experience. It is here where you are most powerful and most vulnerable. It is here where you must be in command.

Setting Your Sights

Setting your sights on the prize is not as difficult as you think, for the effort is not as grand an action as you think you would have to take.

When you envision something new, something different from your normal pattern of thinking you cut into the string of images that is your life. These images are projected by you outward and appear in front of you as if a new and uncalculated future, but this is not true.

The future is merely your projection, and to mold it into what you want it to be, you must begin to string together the new images of and about life in your mind. Your current thoughts, the images you present consist of images of debt, illness, broken relationships, mishaps, stress, confusion, and frustration.

Begin to plant images of wealth and abundance, loving, solid relationships, incredible health, and confidence, gratitude, and appreciation. As often as you do this, consider them in a way that they are present now, not that you are trying to change anything that is already manifest.

As you do this, you will begin to see resulting effects appear in your experience.

It is that simple, but you must believe in the process and claim that which you are projecting out. Know that it is there. Trust that it is there until you, at a point, are certain that the starting point of your life is you. Once you believe it, see it clearly in your experience, and begin to take responsibility for every area of your life, a new path will begin to unfold for you.

Revealing the Obvious

The obvious is that all the while, your thinking has been right in front of you. It reveals the motivation for your emotions. It is the cement for your beliefs, habits, your guiding ideas, and these beliefs do not change unless you change them.

If you watch your fellow man/woman they go about their day experiencing the same types of things over and over again and they do not know why. They meet with angry circumstances, they meet with happy circumstances. They meet and hang out with people who are similar to them on the inside, and this is inevitable.

Who you are in the inside, your habitual way of thinking and feeling is what links you to a portion of the world, the universe. It is what links you to certain types of people who think, feel, and behave in certain ways. It is what links you to the exciting times and the misfortunes that you repeatedly, continue to experience.

Life is not rocket science. It is very predictable if you know what the indicators are. If you know what the magnifiers are. If you know what the initiators are.

Each human being's life is a perfect reflection of who they are on the inside. There is no denying it.

If you change what and how you think and feel in any area for a period of time the results of that effort will begin to appear.

A different type of person will show up in your life. You will come in contact with a resource for greater health. You will come in contact with a source or opportunity to experience greater finances. You will come in contact with how to control or change your mental attitude.

Whatever area you focus on is where you should look for the changes, because the results are specific.

Your thoughts of greater health are not going to yield increased finances.

Each thought is specific to certain area of your life and therefore its result is specific to that area.

The Work of the Mind

The workings of the mind are the asphalt, the foundation to life as you know it. It contains the seeds of the highs and lows, the successes and the failures. These seeds grow until they blossom into your experience, alive with the food of your focus.

There is no way of blocking the process except to change your focus. You must change the images of the mind. You must change the emotions that cross the heart. The sights, sounds, smells, and tastes that are imagined, coupled with the inner dialog that communicates the overall possibility of the idea are the buffers, the pieces of the puzzle that fit together nicely in the creation of your experience.

To begin noticing the operations of the mind when you are not thinking is to begin seeing the causes. Patterns of worry, patterns of doubt, patterns of guilt, shame, and embarrassment all stem from reoccurring themes of images that cause you to replay events that are long in your past. You relive these events perfectly in your mind, you feel the emotions, you hear the conversations, you smell the smells, you taste the tastes, and you do everything within your control to perfectly re-create those same types of occurrences, situations, circumstances, and encounters in your future.

Anything you repeatedly think, feel, talk about, and represent in your mind through image you are projecting into your future, giving life as it hurls toward, materializing in this physical realm.

Everything, everything, everything, you see in your mind first.

From vacations, to going to work, to going to school, to your interactions with people, your partners and your children, to going to the bathroom; you see it in your mind first.

It is subtle. It is quick. It is your only true place of control, no matter how much you try to exert yourself on the world outside of you. It is the place, the part of you that you know the least. It is the place where you are meant to be under control.

You are a magnificent vessel. You are a spiritual being who is human, with the power to move energy on a subatomic level, and combine these particles through the activities of your thinking until they manifest in your experience as events and encounters, and you are doing it all the time without ceasing.

The Change That Follows

The change that follows has been touched upon throughout this book. It is the natural progression of every human being who thinks.

It is because of the fact that you do not remember your thinking process that you do not recognize the reflective nature and precision of your life to your thinking that you continue moving in a haze of confusion, frustration, and willingly playing the role of the victim to outside forces.

The types of people that we meet are a reflection of the inner nature that we project into the world. The types of situations that we encounter are a reflection of the inner nature that we project into the universe. Reoccurring events in our lives are a reflection of the images that have been installed into your unconscious mind. Experiences good and bad are the result of a focus of the mind on those experiences. The only way for you to escape it is for someone to tell you directly, and offer you the opportunity to decide for yourself how you want to approach life with your new found power.

It is up to you.

In your choosing, I hope you choose wisely. Take the power, the reins of your experience and steer them off your current path. Focus on the things that you want, the experiences that you want, for the other factors follow a proper focus. Hold on to your focus long enough to take into account everything that begins to happen in your life directly related to that focus. You can literally watch the changes occur.

These are a few parables of life. I hope they serve as guidance for you along the way, as you begin to carve out a new path of existence for you no matter which way your road may turn. Remember, the trusting timber serves and protects the monkey even when it doesn't know the monkey is there. This is the work of the mind.

Gracias (Spanish)

About Benny

Benny Ferguson Jr., once a weary traveler, feeling completely helpless to life, has suffered paralyzing fear, low levels of self-worth and depression, and contemplated suicide. He has attempted and failed, time after time, to achieve and succeed in his finances, his health, and his personal relationships, but always fell victim to unknown fears, self-sabotaging behaviors, limits and barriers.

His personal struggle culminated in 2005, with him waking up at 1:30 am in an angry rage. He woke up after a fear based dream, similar to the ones he had experienced dating back to elementary school, which forced him into an out-of-body experience. From that point he knew that there was more to life than he had previously been taught and ever knew was possible.

His search for an understanding of who he was, what he was capable of, and how to correct the unknown fears and barriers within, led him to the major spiritual traditions of the world (Teachings of Jesus, Buddhism, Hinduism, The Tao, Islam), branches of Psychology, and to Quantum Physics.

The Result:

"The Diamond Mind Approach to Life and Business,"

Where Benny ventures to explain and help human beings become aware for themselves (REMEMBER), that each individual is creating their own life experience through the images they hold as beliefs (unconsciously), their thoughts and their emotions.

Life is being lived from the inside out, and the moment we begin to live life from this understanding we realize that it is true.

"The Diamond Mind Approach to Life and Business" explains:

Life

- Why and how life is being lived from the inside out;
- How to become aware of your thoughts and their continuous manifestation;
- How to take control of the Core Inner Processes, the nonphysical faculties that are the fundamental starting point to life (beliefs, thoughts, emotions);
- How to begin observing and become aware of the subtle changes, materializations and manifestations, that occur as a result of your inner work;
- How to develop a **Diamond Mind** that does not compromise with life.

Business

- How to manage and take control of the mind of your business or organization;
- How the mind of your business and your employees is sabotaging skill and potential;
- How a **Diamond Mind** frees you and your employees of preexisting programming that hinders approaching maximum performance, production, and potential;
- Why/How no less than a **Diamond Mind** in Leadership, Sales, Customer Service and Organizational Culture should be accepted.

Connecting With Benny:

Facebook: www.facebook.com/bennyrfergusonjr

Youtube: www.youtube.com/BennyFergusonJr/videos

Twitter: www.twitter.com/BennyRFergusonJ

Contacting Benny:

Initial contacts to Benny for discussions, interviews, one – on - one or group coaching, speaking or training may be made through telephone or email.

Phone: 336-546-7142

Email: BennyFerguson@TheFergusonCompany.com